CHEATED

WHAT TO DO WHEN LIFE'S NOT FAIR

JERRY JONES

CHEATED

WHAT TO DO WHEN LIFE'S NOT FAIR

CHEATED

by Jerry Jones

© 2007 Word Aflame Press
Hazelwood, MO 63042

Printed in United States of America

WORD AFLAME PRESS
8855 Dunn Road, Hazelwood, MO 63042
www.pentecostalpublishing.com

Library of Congress Cataloging-in-Publication Data

Jones, Jerry, 1952-
    Cheated : what to do when life's not fair / Jerry Jones.
      p. cm.
    ISBN 978-1-56722-710-9
    1. Bible. O.T. Genesis—Criticism, interpretation, etc. 2. Fairness. 3. Leah (Biblical matriarch) 4. Jacob (Biblical partiarch) I. Title.
BS1235.52.J66 2007
222'.1106—dc22   2007015362

FOR MY WIFE AND SON

TABLE OF CONTENTS

PREFACE

This book is an attempt to answer one of the fundamental questions of the human experience: what do you do when life is unfair? I am aware that this is an ambitious task. I can only excuse the brashness of even attempting to answer such a question by this disclaimer: I do not pretend to have the answer. But I am convinced that God does and that He has given us the answer in His Book, the Bible. I am only pointing you to a story in that Book where I think the answer can be found.

I have made some assumptions that might need explaining. I have assumed that you will translate the incidents that are described in this book into the circumstances of your own life. You may not have been cheated by life in the same way as Leah, but cheated nevertheless. I pray that by seeing Leah's life through the prism of your own experience, you will learn something from Leah's pain and her reaction to it.

I also assume you will grant me the liberty to "flesh out" the characters in this old story. I have often wished we knew more about the men and women we meet in the pages of the Bible. How did they feel; what did they think; how did they react to life during those times when the record is silent? We can only guess about these things, and I readily confess I have done some guessing. But I have tried to keep my suppositions as close to the biblical narrative as possible, only describing what, in my opinion, could logically be assumed from what we know. You may disagree with some or all of my assumptions, and I understand, but I hope you will be helped and blessed anyway.

I owe a lot of people for the inspiration behind this book, all the way back (way, way back) to my Bible quizzing days, when Genesis—all fifty chapters—was the book of study one year. My study of Leah and her life was sparked by a sermon I read somewhere more than fifteen years ago. (I cannot be sure where and, after an exhaustive search, can't locate that sermon now. I apologize to the writer and wish to acknowledge him or her). Several years later, Pastor Jonathan Urshan preached on Leah and her sons at a chapel service at World Evangelism Center, headquarters of the United Pentecostal Church. His message greatly added to my knowledge and appreciation of this story.

I also must acknowledge those who, when I have preached on Leah's journey from pain to praise, encouraged me to write this book.

I am indebted to all these folks and so many more.

INTRODUCTION

These things I have spoken unto you, that in me ye might have peace. In the world ye shall have tribulation: but be of good cheer; I have overcome the world (John 16:33).

Life isn't fair. It is not negative to say so; it is simply realistic. All of our experiences teach us this is true. We see the innocent suffer while the wicked prosper; we watch hard work go unnoticed while sloth is rewarded. In our society, the unimportant is heralded while the truly valuable is discounted. When we realize this, or especially when we experience it in our own lives, we sometimes feel that our experience is unique. We search for reasons in our society, our government, our times. But injustice is not new, nor is it unique to us. Four thousand years ago in the Book of Ecclesiastes, a preacher wrote:

I returned, and saw under the sun, that the race is not to the swift, nor the battle to the strong, neither yet bread to the wise, nor yet riches to men of understanding, nor yet favour to men of skill; but time and chance happeneth to them all (Ecclesiastes 9:11).

The key statement is in the final phrase "to them all." The only fairness about life is that it is unfair to everyone. No one escapes its injustice: the rich, the poor, the good, the bad, those who try, and those who don't. There is unfairness for all. The most fortunate, the most blessed, the ones who never seem to struggle, all taste the same bitterness. For if no other misfortune ever befalls a person, his life and his accomplishments will still end in the grave.

It is ironic that the tragedies that make up the unfairness of life are only part of the story. Loss, sickness, trouble in the family, financial struggles, and a thousand other calamities people deal with are made infinitely worse when they are undeserved; that is, when they happen to us with little rhyme or reason, when they make no sense. The outrage that comes from suffering innocently magnifies the pain.

This is what makes the Book of Job timeless. It is not just that Job suffered loss. Although the short space of time in which it happened combined with the completeness of his tragedy take our breath, the true poignancy of Job's trial is that it was completely undeserved.

There was a man in the land of Uz, whose name was Job: and that man was perfect and upright, and one that feared God, and eschewed evil (Job 1:1).

And the LORD said unto Satan, Hast thou considered my ser-
vant Job, that there is none like him in the earth, a perfect and an
upright man, one that feareth God, and escheweth evil? (Job 1:8).

To us, a man so described should have a life of nothing but the blessings of God. Earning such praise from the Lord Himself puts to rest any chance that the terrible calamities that came to Job were in any way because of his own mistakes or shortcomings. He was innocent, yet he suffered horribly. The story of Job was the story of life at its worst. It was also the story of mankind at his best. Even though driven to frustration by the injustice of his suffering and the insensitive accusations of his "friends," Job endured and overcame because he maintained his integrity by not "[sinning] with his lips," "nor [charging] God foolishly."

Most of us will never suffer the loss that Job did; but that doesn't mean we are not deeply affected by the unfairness we encounter in our lives. Even relatively insignificant losses produce the same emotional turmoil as more serious injustice. Several years ago I read of a poll taken by the Gallup Organization. Although better known for their political polling, the Gallup Organization also poll in other areas of American life: religion, economics, relationships, and so forth. Periodically, they complete one master poll in which they attempt to acquire a picture of what everyday life is like for the people who live in the United States. The focus of this poll is not the big issues of life but the little things. They try to identify the ordinary, seemingly insignificant aspects of daily existence that, taken together, make life what it really is.

In one such poll, a question was designed to determine the most frustrating things that Americans deal with in their everyday lives. Some answers to the question are predictable: slow drivers, shoddy products, oversleeping. However, it is unexpected and very revealing that the majority of Americans polled say they feel most frustrated in their everyday lives when they put money in a Coke machine, punch the button, and nothing comes out.

I can relate to this frustration. Once, while at a hotel, I was thirsty and went to the cold drink machine to purchase a soda. I put in my $1.50 and punched the Diet Coke button. Out came a root beer. That was frustrating. I didn't want a root beer; I wanted a Diet Coke. I stood there with this undrinkable root beer in my hand and I thought, *If the Diet Coke button gave me a root beer, then maybe the root beer button will give me a Diet Coke.* Unfortunately, I did not have any more change, so I went all the way down to the front desk to break a five-dollar bill, came all the way back up, put in my money, and punched the root beer button. And sure enough, a root beer came out.

Why are such relatively unimportant things so frustrating to us? Even if it is $1.50 a can, it's not really the money. What is it that "bugs" us about putting our money in and not getting our Diet Coke out?

It is simply this: the most frustrating part of life is when I do my part and I don't get what I deserve. It does not matter if it is a cold drink machine, a paycheck at the end of the week, or a lifetime of hard work. There is something about not getting treated fairly, not getting what I deserve, that cruelly piles frustration upon my pain. The size of the slight is not important; being cheated is.

And what about when it is not the small things that cheat us? What about when it is life itself that robs us of what is rightfully ours? What about when life not only refuses to give us what we deserve, but—to add insult to injury—gives it to someone else?

What do I do when I try as hard as anyone else and am not rewarded as others? What do I do when my job is sent overseas and I am sent home? What do I do when those I love break my heart and there is simply no way to fix it? What do I do when life is unfair, when it gives me not what I deserve, but what I don't deserve?

What should you do when you've been cheated? I believe I know a place where the answer to this important question can be found.

I want to tell you a story from the Bible.

JACOB THE CHEATER

And Isaac was forty years old when he took Rebekah to wife, the daughter of Bethuel the Syrian of Padan-aram, the sister to Laban the Syrian. And Isaac intreated the LORD for his wife, because she was barren: and the LORD was intreated of him, and Rebekah his wife conceived. And the children struggled together within her; and she said, If it be so, why am I thus? And she went to inquire of the LORD. And the LORD said unto her, Two nations are in thy womb, and two manner of people shall be separated from thy bowels; and the one people shall be stronger than the other people; and the elder shall serve the younger. And when her days to be delivered were fulfilled, behold, there were twins in her womb (Genesis 25:20-24).

CHAPTER I

TWINS

Excitement filled the tents of Isaac. After years of longing and praying for a child, he and Rebekah were going to have a baby! For months, the only question on the minds of the entire household—servants, shepherds, herdsmen, and all their families—had been: will it be a son or a daughter? Recently, news swept through the camp that God had revealed to Rebekah that she would have twin boys; then came the equally exciting report that the midwives, after watching Rebekah's pregnancy and carefully considering all the signs, had agreed. But of course, until the child—or children—was born, no one could really be sure. So anticipation grew day after day, reaching a peak when finally Rebekah went into labor. Throughout that day, servants whispered their predictions, midwives rushed about barking orders, and Isaac paced nervously just outside the tent.

It *was* twin boys, and they were born only moments apart. But those few seconds made all the difference for them, making one son the elder, granting him all the inheritance, and leaving the younger son, although born only moments after his brother, with nothing.

The first-born was named Esau, a name that means "hairy," because he was born covered with fine red hair. The second-born son was named Jacob in a startlingly prophetic act. *Jacob* means "supplanter." A supplanter is one who takes the place of another without a right to do so. No doubt he was named this because of a striking event that occurred during the brothers' births. When Jacob emerged from his mother's womb, just after Esau, he reached up and grasped the heel of his brother. This reflexive action by a newborn captured an important aspect of his nature. He would always be reaching for more, grasping every opportunity to catch up with and ultimately surpass his brother.

Their natures reflected this struggle. Esau was rough and rebellious. He always chose his own path, sometimes deliberately rejecting the teaching and advice of his parents, going his own way even when it was the wrong way. He spent long, lonely hours hunting in the fields and woods. He had little patience or appreciation for domestic pursuits. The stories his father told of Abraham and Sarah and their epic, God-inspired journey from Ur in faraway Mesopotamia to this Promised Land seemed to Esau unimportant, even slightly ridiculous. The tale about his grandfather taking his father up a mountain and almost sacrificing him had a certain fascination about it, but all that talk about destiny and calling and covenant bored him. Give him a good bow, a strong, straight arrow, and a buck in his sights; those were all he cared about!

Jacob was very different. He never cared much for hunting or sports or any of the other rough-and-tumble pursuits of the other boys, including his brother. He preferred to spend time around the house, learning how to handle a household and a business. He was very close to his mother, and they spent hours together. He never got enough of her accounts of her childhood in Haran.

He revered his father, and never tired of listening to him recount the stories of the journey he and his father, Abraham, made to Moriah, where God commanded Abraham to offer Isaac as a human sacrifice, only to intervene at the last second, and explain that it had been a test of Abraham's faithfulness, or of the physical visitation of God on the plains of Mamre, or of the destruction of Sodom and Gommorah because not even ten righteous people could be found there. He would lie awake at night and wonder at the promises the Lord had made to his grandfather and father, and the responsibilities those promises placed on his family.

There was no doubt in Jacob's mind that they were special; his family was a destined people, chosen by God for some vast purpose. Something in him longed to have not a bit part but a star role in the drama of history. He would give anything to be named in the line of patriarchal succession, anything to make it not Abraham, Isaac, and Esau, as it seemed destined to be, but Abraham, Isaac, and Jacob.

However, his birth order prevented this. He was the second born, if only by seconds. It just seemed so unfair.

It would be a mistake to think that because Jacob spent time around the house instead of the woods that he was weak or even mild-mannered. The truth was that Jacob was driven. This drive, embedded in his nature, would dominate his young life and pit Jacob against his brother almost from the beginning. Unfortunately, because of it, he would do almost anything to reach his goals. Jacob's entire character was shaped by this drive, his every action scribed by it. Everything he did had a calculation about it, an underlying cunning that revealed a hunger to take what belonged to his brother by any means possible. When dealing with Jacob, Esau soon learned that everything had a price and every favor an ulterior motive; even a bowl of soup required a payment.

One day, Esau came home from a hunt to find Jacob preparing a pot of bean soup. Esau hadn't eaten all day, and the aroma of the soup reminded him of it. Suddenly he was famished, weak from his hunger. "Give me some of your soup, brother," he said. "I am about to faint, I am so hungry."

Jacob looked up at Esau, his hand continuing to stir the pot with a wooden spoon. His face became almost feral, and a cunning look formed around his eyes. "I will, but it will cost you."

"How much?" Esau was cautious, suspicious.

*A*nd Abram fell on his face: and God talked with him, saying, As for me, behold, my covenant is with thee, and thou shalt be a father of many nations. Neither shall thy name any more be called Abram, but thy name shall be Abraham; for a father of many nations have I made thee. And I will make thee exceeding fruitful, and I will make nations of thee, and kings shall come out of thee. And I will establish my covenant between me and thee and thy seed after thee in their generations for an everlasting covenant, to be a God unto thee, and to thy seed after thee. And I will give unto thee, and to thy seed after thee, the land wherein thou art a stranger, all the land of Canaan, for an everlasting possession; and I will be their God (Genesis 17:3-8).

"The birthright. Sell me your birthright."

It was hard to imagine that Jacob was serious. The birthright was Esau's place in the line of succession. It was what guaranteed that he would inherit his father's vast estate, a fortune in sheep, cattle, and land. Jacob was asking Esau to give him all this in return for a bowl of soup.

But Jacob had recognized a weakness in his brother. There was a cockiness about him, a macho posturing that advertised his sense of disdain for other people and, Jacob realized, a disdain aimed particularly at their father.

Esau thought Isaac was weak. He laughed at his father's timidity for claiming that the lovely Rebekah was not his wife but his sister when he was afraid someone would kill him and take her. No real man would have done such a thing. And what about when Isaac had grown richer and more powerful than anyone around, and because of local envy the Philistine king Abimelech had ordered Isaac out of Philistia? Rather than resist, Isaac had meekly retreated. And that whole rigmarole about wrangling over those wells Isaac had dug. Esau wouldn't have put up with those impertinent herdsmen in Gerar, not for a minute. He would have put them in their place—flat on their backs. Oh, yes, no doubt Isaac was a weak man.

Jacob was determined to exploit this immature opinion Esau

held of Isaac, and something told him this was the right moment. After he made the offer to sell the soup for the birthright, he could almost follow Esau's thoughts: the birthright, yes, it was great, a fortune, really. But what of it? It had been built by Isaac, a weak man. If *he* could build so great a fortune, how much of a greater one could Esau build for himself? He didn't need his father's riches. Let Jacob have it all. Esau would show them what a strong man, a real man could do.

Jacob quietly kept tending the soup pot, waiting for Esau to rationalize away his inheritance. Finally, Esau spoke, expressing the least rational reason of all to sell his birthright: "Well, I'm starving to death," he said. "What good is a fortune to a dead man?"

Jacob could hardly believe his ears. He had schemed, planned, and hoped for this moment for so long that it was hard to believe it had finally come. "Do you swear it?" he asked Esau.

"I swear," Esau replied. Jacob smiled as he filled a bowl with the bean soup and handed it to his brother.

Thus Esau despised his birthright (Genesis 25:34).

Follow peace with all men, and holiness, without which no man shall see the Lord: looking diligently lest any man fail of the grace of God; lest any root of bitterness springing up trouble you, and thereby many be defiled; lest there be any fornicator, or profane person, as Esau, who for one morsel of meat sold his birthright. For ye know how that afterward, when he would have inherited the blessing, he was rejected: for he found no place of repentance, though he sought it carefully with tears (Hebrews 12:14-17).

THE BLESSING

Even after the purchase of Esau's birthright, Jacob's obsession would not let him rest. There was one last step necessary to complete the campaign to achieve complete ascendancy over his brother. Jacob's drive toward this goal culminated in a scheme, hatched with his mother's connivance, to deceive his father and steal his brother's blessing.

The blessing was an ancient ceremony of transfer and confirmation. The father, by laying his hands upon his firstborn son and pronouncing a blessing upon him, symbolically transferred his spiritual inheritance to him. It was a final confirmation to the community that the leadership of the family, as well as the wealth of the father, had been passed to the son. When Rebekah overheard Isaac sending Esau to hunt a deer and prepare a venison stew, she knew what it meant; the long struggle Jacob had waged to supplant his brother as heir and successor to Isaac would be for naught. The blessing would once and for all transfer the inheritance to Esau.

In a panic, Rebekah went to Jacob, explained what was about to happen, and instructed him to impersonate his brother and deceive his blind father into blessing the wrong son. Their ruse, even though it was so clumsy even the blind Isaac had misgivings, worked. It took some fancy footwork, a little lying, and some fleece on his arms and neck (you have to wonder just how hairy *was* Esau?), but in the end, Jacob felt his father's hands on his head and heard the blessing pronounced over him.

As Jacob hurriedly left his father's tent before Esau could return from the hunt, he must have exulted in his final victory over his brother. He probably had no idea of the calamity he had just set in motion. This ultimate act of betrayal would bring tremendous changes in Jacob's family and in his own life.

When Esau discovered what Jacob had done, he was brokenhearted:

> *And he said, Is not he rightly named Jacob? for he hath supplanted me these two times: he took away my birthright; and, behold, now he hath taken away my blessing. And he said, Hast thou not reserved a blessing for me? And Isaac answered and said unto Esau, Behold, I have made him thy lord, and all his brethren have I given to him for servants; and with corn and wine have I sustained him: and what shall I do now unto thee, my son? And Esau said unto his father, Hast thou but one blessing, my father? bless me, even me also, O my father. And Esau lifted up his voice, and wept* (Genesis 27:36-38).

But Esau's tears and his plaintive cry for the blessing soon gave way to rage against the brother who had done this to him. His anger was so great he vowed to kill Jacob as soon as their father passed away and the obligatory days of mourning were completed.

Hearing of Esau's vow, Rebekah, desperate to save her favorite son's life, determined that Jacob must go away. She thought of her hometown in a region called Padan-aram. Living with her relatives, she reasoned, Jacob would be safe from Esau's murderous wrath. It is likely Rebekah planned that after a few months Esau would forget his vow, and Jacob could safely return home. But when she sent him away in a panic, almost certainly without a farewell to his father, she did not know that this farewell was final.

Jacob's life of comfort as the son of a wealthy and powerful man was over. Carrying only a few provisions, he kissed his mother good-bye and ran for his life.

THE ENCOUNTER

Jacob plunged into the wilderness, alone. He had never been the outdoorsman his brother was, so he was in unfamiliar surroundings. After a long, tiring first day of travel, a day filled with the fear that Esau would overtake him, Jacob found a sheltered place to spend the night. The shadows grew around him as he spread a blanket on the ground and found a rock to serve for his pillow. There followed a night of uneasy sleep.

As he slept, Jacob dreamed. In his dream he saw an astonishing sight. A ladder stood on the earth and stretched into heaven, and as he watched, angels ascended and descended the ladder. At the top stood the Lord. If this sight surprised Jacob, the words the Lord spoke must have astonished him.

> *I am the LORD God of Abraham thy father, and the God of Isaac: the land whereon thou liest, to thee will I give it, and to thy seed; and thy seed shall be as the dust of the earth, and thou shalt spread abroad to the west, and to the east, and to the north, and to the south: and in thee and in thy seed shall all the families of the earth be blessed. And, behold, I am with thee, and will keep thee in all places whither thou goest, and will bring thee again into this land; for I will not leave thee, until I have done that which I have spoken to thee of* (Genesis 28:13-15).

God was renewing the covenant He had established with Jacob's grandfather, Abraham, and with his father, Isaac. God, it seemed, was confirming that the birthright and the blessing had indeed been transferred not to the elder son but rather to the younger.

Did this mean that God placed His approval on Jacob and Rebekah's scheming and lying to Isaac and on Jacob's lifetime of effort to cheat his brother out of that which was rightfully his? Not at all.

Jacob did not steal his brother's birthright as much as Esau deserted it, leaving it for his ambitious brother to claim. His attitude of rebellion and disdain for the things of God disqualified him to wear the mantle of his grandfather and father. The first manifestation of this flaw in Esau's attitude toward God was made clear when he sold the birthright to Jacob for a bowl of bean soup.

Then Jacob gave Esau bread and pottage of lentiles; and he did eat and drink, and rose up, and went his way: thus Esau despised his birthright (Genesis 25:34).

This despising of the things of God became a pattern in Esau's life, a habit of thought that he followed until it was too late. The writer of Hebrews used the tragedy of Esau as a warning to all those who do not value the eternal over the earthly.

> *Lest there be any fornicator, or profane person, as Esau, who for one morsel of meat sold his birthright. For ye know how that afterward, when he would have inherited the blessing, he was rejected: for he found no place of repentance, though he sought it carefully with tears* (Hebrews 12:16-17).

What happened to Esau was of his own doing.

This does not mean that Jacob was blameless or that God overlooked the flaws in his character. Jacob was chosen not because he was worthy but because he chose the things of God above all else in his life. He valued the ways of God as much as Esau despised them. This is why Jacob received the birthright and the blessing; he loved the God of his fathers, and God honored that love.

Although God loved Jacob, He would not leave him as he was. As Jacob broke camp the next morning, his heart was filled with wonder at the dream and its promises. "Surely the LORD is in this place; and I knew it not," he exclaimed. The rock that had been his pillow became a pillar marking the place where he had first experienced the presence of God. He called the place Bethel: "The House of God."

He continued his journey to Padan-aram, filled with a new sense of purpose. Soon, he would arrive at his new home, and there Jacob would discover a new love and a whole new life.

But first, the cheater would find out how it felt to be cheated.

RACHEL AND LEAH

And Laban had two daughters: the name of the elder was Leah, and the name of the younger was Rachel. Leah was tender eyed; but Rachel was beautiful and well favoured. And Jacob loved Rachel; and said, I will serve thee seven years for Rachel thy younger daughter. And Laban said, It is better that I give her to thee, than that I should give her to another man: abide with me. And Jacob served seven years for Rachel; and they seemed unto him but a few days, for the love he had to her (Genesis 29:16-20).

CHAPTER 2

RACHEL

The story of Jacob and Rachel is one of the great romances of all time. It began when Jacob, fleeing Esau's anger, arrived in the land to which his mother had sent him. It was Rebekah's home, the area where Jacob's grandfather, Abraham, had lived for a time on the journey from Ur of the Chaldees to Canaan. Rebekah believed Jacob would be safe from Esau there and that her family would take him in and look after him.

When Jacob first arrived in the East, he came to a field where three flocks of sheep lay scattered around a well. The shepherds were waiting for the agreed-upon time to move the heavy capstone from the top of the well so they could water their flocks. Jacob immediately approached the shepherds and asked where they lived. When they answered Haran, Jacob recognized the name of his mother's hometown and asked if they knew Laban, his mother's brother. "We do," was the reply, "and in fact, there is his daughter, Rachel." When Jacob turned and saw beautiful Rachel leading a flock of sheep toward the well, it was love at first sight.

What occurred next is an ironic reversal from the story (no doubt well-known to both Jacob and Rachel) of the meeting between Jacob's mother, Rebekah, and Eliezer, the servant Abraham had sent to find a suitable bride for Isaac his son. Then, it was Rebekah who proved she was to be Isaac's bride by drawing water from a well, perhaps this very one, and watering Eliezer's camels.

This time, Jacob moved the stone and, although it was not the traditional time of day to do so, watered Rachel's flock. Rachel ran to tell her father, Laban, of the arrival of his sister's son, and Laban hurried to meet Jacob. He extravagantly welcomed Jacob and invited him to stay with them as long as he remained in Haran.

Laban may not have known that Jacob had already fallen in love with Rachel, but after about a month, he found out in a dramatic way. Talking with Jacob, Laban asked him about his plans for the future. Jacob had been lending a hand with Laban's farm operations, and impressed with the young man, Laban urged him to remain in Haran and take a job working with Laban's flocks and herds. When Jacob told Laban that he was very interested in the offer, Laban asked what wages he would require. Jacob answered, "I will work for you for seven years if your daughter Rachel will become my wife."

It is difficult to find a more impressive expression of love than this. Without a doubt, Jacob deeply loved Laban's younger daughter. Imagine working for seven years with no wages, no hope of advancement, nothing except room and board and the promise that Rachel will

Eleazar was Abraham's chief steward or servant. He was probably the servant sent by Abraham to pick out a bride for his son, Isaac. When Eleazar arrived at the village of Haran, he prayed for divine guidance in selecting the right girl for Isaac. His prayer was simple: whichever young woman would reveal a kind and generous heart by drawing water from the well and giving his thirsty camels a drink would be the one he should take back to Canaan. When asked, Rebekah cheerfully watered the camels, no easy job, and thus was chosen to be Isaac's wife. Jacob, no doubt aware of this event and knowing that Rachel would also know of it, watered her flock as a statement of his instant love for her and his desire to become her husband.

at the end of the seven years become your wife. That is love!

Laban must have been stunned. He could hardly believe his good fortune. A shrewd businessman, he quickly calculated the numbers. Even though the beautiful Rachel would command a good dowry, certainly it would be nothing compared to seven years of unpaid labor from the young, intelligent, obviously strong Jacob. Laban never thought twice about taking advantage of this boy who had come to him for shelter and help. There was money to be made, and Laban intended to make it.

Although delighted, Laban struggled to hide his joy. He did not want to appear eager to make the arrangement, afraid Jacob would come to his senses and change his mind, causing this incredible deal to slip through his greedy fingers. "Well," he replied, pretending to debate the proposal, "it is better to give her to you rather than to some other man. All right, I'll do it."

For seven years, Jacob lived with Laban, working day after day, tending livestock, developing pasture, preparing for the winter months, making Laban richer and richer and all the while receiving nothing for himself. The story must have spread throughout Padan-aram. Some wondered at a love so great that a man would labor seven years for the woman he loved, while others snickered at the naiveté of the young man from Canaan willing to work seven years for free when, no doubt, if he had made a fair wage, he could have paid Rachel's dowry with money to spare. Still others, shaking their heads at that wily Laban, wondered how he so completely pulled the wool over that boy's eyes. Yet, even if he heard the gossip, Jacob did not care. For him the seven years of labor passed as if they were only a few days.

Eventually, the long anticipated day arrived. Seven years of his life and labor had been completed; Laban's contract had been fulfilled. Jacob had given what was required without complaint. He had done what was expected of him, and the seven years had come and gone. Now he was going to make Rachel his bride. His wedding day had come.

LEAH

It is difficult to imagine how the deception could have happened. Possibly Jacob overindulged himself with wine at the wedding festivities. Perhaps it was something as simple as the darkness of the nuptial tent. Whatever the explanation, Jacob awoke the morning after his wedding to discover that he was not married to Rachel; he was married to her older sister, Leah. The ungainly details of Laban's scheme—sneaking Leah into Jacob's tent, assuring the distraught Rachel to be patient (it would work out, wait and see, she would still be Jacob's wife)—made it even harder to believe the ruse could have been successful. Yet it was. After working seven long years, Jacob was married to the wrong woman.

While it is hard to imagine how Laban pulled off the matrimonial bluff, it is not hard to picture Jacob's anger and indignation as he stormed into his father-in-law's tent.

"You cheated me!" he shouted. "I worked seven years for Rachel, not for Leah! I don't love Leah!"

Laban was ready with his response. "But, Jacob, you should know I have no choice." He spread his hands, a look of innocent reasonableness on his face. "In our country, a father cannot give away a younger daughter until the older is first married. It simply isn't done. I have tried to find a husband for Leah but failed. I continued my efforts until the last possible moment, but as no one wanted Leah, I did all I could think of to do: I gave her to you."

Jacob saw through Laban's flimsy excuse. He had lived and worked in Haran for more than seven years. Why would he not have been told of this tradition before now, unless his father-in-law had planned this ruse from the beginning? And what was Laban's purpose in all this?

It became obvious with his next words. Laban stood, placed a fatherly hand on Jacob's shoulder, and with a conciliatory smile said, "But there is no reason you can't still have Rachel. Just work for me for seven more years, and I'll give her to you, too."

Jacob was seething, but he could not undo the wedding night. He struck the deal and went through the week-long wedding festivities with a woman he did not love, all the while keeping his anger in check by reminding himself that Rachel would be his.

It seems likely that Jacob did not have to wait seven more years to marry Rachel. Probably because Laban knew Jacob's word was good, that if he had promised to work seven more years he would do so, Laban agreed to an immediate wedding between Jacob and Rachel. Having gotten what he wanted, he saw no advantage to himself to make them wait. So Jacob and Rachel wed.

This tragic scheme left all three young people wounded. Laban's selfishness and greed would scar each of them for the rest of their days. This one act would shape their lives and the lives of their children for decades to come. They were all cheated.

Jacob was cheated. For the rest of his life, he would be married to a woman he did not love. Every time he looked at Leah, he would remember Laban's treachery, the seven years he had been tricked into working without pay for her. This is no doubt why the Bible tells us that Jacob not only did not love Leah but hated her; she reminded him that he had been cheated.

Rachel was cheated. She would forever share the man she loved with her big sister. She slept alone on the wedding night for which she had planned seven years. Even the first ceremony in which she had no doubt participated was little more than a cruel joke. The second wedding a week later was a hurried affair in comparison.

She had to endure the fact that she, her sister, and her new husband were the talk of the land. Snide remarks, whispered jokes, and amused glances followed them everywhere they went. Worst of all, her home became a battleground, not between her and her husband, for Jacob truly and deeply loved her; but her marriage became an endless struggle with Leah. Their competition for Jacob's attention consumed them both.

While Jacob and Rachel were both cheated by Laban's greed and selfishness, the greatest victim in this tragedy was Leah. Leah has often been passed over in this story as if it wasn't also her story. Sometimes she has even been treated as an object of ridicule. This is because the image of the ugly sister sneaking into the unsuspecting bridegroom's bedroom on his wedding night sounds like some off-color joke. But there is not a hint that Leah had anything to do with the bridal switch that Laban executed on Jacob's wedding night. She was simply a pawn in her father's selfish game.

Surely we can assume that Leah, like nearly every other little girl before and since, had dreamed of her own wedding day when she would be the bride, when she would wear the white dress, when she would walk down the aisle. Even in a time and culture of arranged marriages, surely she imagined her groom standing, waiting for her, his eyes locked on hers and those eyes filled with unmistakable love. She was sure that he would love her and no other all her life.

But that would never happen to Leah. Instead, she married a man who hated her, who never looked at her with love in his eyes, never spoke to her with love in his voice, but always saw her as a reminder of the day her father cheated him. Not only did she live with a man who did not love her, but she was compared every day, in everything she did, with a younger, more beautiful, more vivacious sister. She constantly witnessed her husband's passionate, tender gaze on Rachel, but when his gaze fixed on Leah, the fires of passion died down to burning coals of resentment. She heard him always speak to Rachel with a loving lilt, but when he spoke to Leah, it was a perfunctory monotone. Leah was cheated.

The Bible is brutally honest about so many things, and it certainly is about Leah. It didn't really say that Leah was ugly, but it certainly left that impression. Something about her eyes made her less appealing. But the biggest problem was that she was not Rachel. Jacob loved Rachel. He did not love Leah. It may have been simply that his love for Rachel was so great that it made his love for Leah seem like hatred.

Apparently, however, a very strange insult was added to her injury. Not only was Leah married to a man who hated her, not only was Leah forever condemned to compete with a woman who would outshine her in every way, but Leah suffered a further tragic irony: she fell in love with Jacob. Leah loved Jacob with a deep and enduring love, and this love became the driving force of her life.

Leah never stopped dreaming of the day when she would enter the tent where Jacob was, and he would stop what he was doing, look up with a smile, and greet her with an endearment. She saw it happen again and again with Rachel. It seemed to her that he could not overhear Rachel's voice without stopping and listening. He could not see Rachel walk into a room without stopping whatever he was doing and looking at her in that certain way. Leah dreamed that that day might come for her, and to this dream she dedicated her life.

LEAH'S OBSESSION

Now therefore my husband will love me (Genesis 29:32).

Now this time will my husband be joined unto me, because I have born him three sons (Genesis 29:34).

Hope deferred maketh the heart sick (Proverbs 13:12).

CHAPTER 3

TO BE LOVED BY JACOB

But that day would never come.

Leah made a great mistake. Overwhelmed by the resentment and pain caused by the unfairness of her situation, she allowed her love for Jacob and her desire to gain his love in return to grow into an obsession. She began to think that her life could be fair, her pain ended, and happiness finally obtained, if only she could win Jacob's love. Her entire life focused on this one goal. She determined to make Jacob notice her, appreciate her, and eventually love her. This became the motive for all she did.

She made certain his favorite foods were prepared and that the tent was always clean and orderly. She never dreamed of leaving her bedroom without her hair being perfectly in place and her clothes immaculate. Though she didn't have the beauty of Rachel, she always made sure that Jacob saw her in the best light possible. She tried in every way to be the perfect wife.

It was Leah who always saw to it that meals were served on time, the menu was always to her husband's liking, the children not noisy or bothersome, and the household run quietly and efficiently. These were all admirable efforts, but what made Leah an object of pity instead of admiration was the motive behind all that she did. Keeping the tent neat and clean was more about pleasing Jacob than creating a clean, healthy environment for the whole family. The way she dressed, spoke, and acted was shaped by her need for his approval and love. The goal of her day was to gain an appreciative glance or a kind word from him. When it actually happened, she would lie awake that night almost giddy with delight; when it didn't (as was more often the case), she would lie as stiff and hopeless as a corpse, staring into the tent's gloomy shadows.

But regardless of yesterday's disappointment, she got up every morning, looked in the mirror, and told herself, "If I look as good as I can, if I keep the tent tidy, the children well-behaved, meals like he likes them, then eventually he will see how much I love him and surely then he will love me. And then when he loves me, finally he will look at me like he looks at her. He will say the things to me that he says to her."

The true tragedy of Leah was not her unrequited love for Jacob or her sordid and childish competition with Rachel; it was her surrendering of her self-worth, her sense of her own value, to another person. She so needed Jacob's approval and love that nothing else made her feel needed, useful, or important. Only with Jacob's love

An obsession is an unwelcome, uncontrollable, and persistent idea, thought, image, or emotion that a person cannot help thinking even though it creates significant distress or anxiety.

People with obsessions may find themselves acting in compulsive ways in largely futile attempts to relieve the anxiety associated with their persistent . . . thoughts. Others suffering from obsessions may try very hard to control or ignore them. It is important to note that legitimate worries about daily concerns are not obsessions. Although they can occasionally be carried to obsessive lengths, these concerns can change with circumstances and, in most cases, be controlled. . . . Obsessions relate to problems that most people would consider far removed from normal, daily events and concerns.

—Dean A. Haycock, Ph.D.

would she feel complete; without it she was nothing.

This led to the impasse where obsession always leads: Leah placed her happiness under the control of another person. Jacob controlled her, perhaps without ever even realizing it.

But aren't wives supposed to love their husbands, and husbands their wives? And when you love someone, does not it follow that you want to please him, to see him happy? Absolutely. But Leah's drive to win her husband's love was not totally about Jacob. It was her way of dealing with the unfair circumstances of her marriage and her life. More than forcing Jacob to love her, she was trying to force life to treat her fairly. Surely this is one of humankind's most fruitless efforts, as empty as Quixote's quest and just as exhausting and consuming. To totally cede happiness into the hands of another human being is a sure recipe for disaster.

People change, they fail, they leave, they die. "I can't live without you" is a romantic conceit that may produce a swoon, but it must never become the truth because the unfairness of life may require us to do just that. We dare not ever surrender our self-worth, our sense of value, our happiness, our joy to another human being. It doesn't matter who it is—husband, wife, children, or parents. There is only One whose love we must have in order to have worth and value as a human being. There is only One whose love we must

co.de.pen.dence(co.di.pen´.dens) n. [root ME. dependaunce < OFr. dependance or ML. dependentia < L. dependens].

Also written *co-dependence*. The condition or fact of being codependent; specifically,
a) the tendency to place the needs and wants of others first and to the exclusion of acknowledging one's own,
b) continued investment of self-esteem in the ability to control both oneself and others,
c) anxiety and boundary distortions relating to intimacy and separation,
d) difficulty expressing feelings,
e) excessive worry how others may respond to one's feelings,
f) undue fear of being hurt and/or rejected by others,
g) self-esteem dependent on approval by others,
h) tendency to ignore one's own values and attempt to adhere to the values of others.

have in order to have joy, peace, and happiness. We must never surrender our sense of worth in this world to anyone except Jesus. He loves us, and that should be enough to fill our hearts with joy and our lives with worth.

HAPPINESS GUARANTEED

The Bible said, "Hope deferred maketh the heart sick" (Proverbs 13:12). When we set our heart on something, work determinedly toward it, and refuse to be diverted from the goal, we fully expect to reach it. When we constantly commit ourselves to seeing our dreams come true but are unfairly denied the results of our efforts, our disappointment overshadows everything else. Life becomes bitter and hard.

Surely it is among the greatest tragedies of life for our dreams always to dance just outside our reach. Again and again we almost grasp them, they are almost ours, but at the last moment life snatches them away. That, the Bible said, makes the heart sick.

We have all seen it happen to others and have experienced it in our own lives. Disappointment poisons the spirit, and bitterness and anger are the result. Our shoulders stoop and our heads bow.

*H*ope deferred maketh the heart sick: but when the desire cometh, it is a tree of life (Proverbs 13:12).

The light goes out of our eyes. We do our best and nothing comes of it. We pay our dues and never get the result we deserve. Then it happens over and over again until we find ourselves broken and shattered by the heartache of our lives. Hope deferred makes the heart sick.

But look at the second half of that verse: "But when the desire cometh, it is a tree of life" (Proverbs 13:12). When the effort we make brings the result we deserve, life takes on a whole different aura: we are fulfilled, we feel successful, and our lives seem to make sense. This happiness affects every part of our lives. Our attitude is better, and optimism replaces discouragement. In other words, life seems fair, and this sense of being treated justly produces happiness.

A simpler, more direct way of saying what the proverb writer was telling us in Proverbs 13:12 is this: when I get what I want I am happy; when I don't get what I want I am not happy. This is as dead-on a description of the human psyche as any ever penned. This accurately describes us from the cradle to the grave.

But it is more than just a statement about us; it is a lesson on how to be happy. The lesson is as simple as it is profound: I must be careful what I desire. If I desire things I cannot have, I condemn myself to a life of bitterness, anger, and heartache. But if I desire only what I can have, then I give myself a life of fulfillment, joy, and happiness.

We literally decide whether we will be happy when we decide what we want. Discussing the frustrations that come with modern materialism and consumerism, Richard Foster in his book, *Freedom of Simplicity*,[1] pointed out that contentment is not found in having more but in wanting less. The world plays a cruel joke on people when it convinces them that "you can have it all." This philosophy only produces happy endings in the make-believe world of novels and movies. In real life we have to make choices, and every choice we make closes the door to a thousand others. This is life. It is lived within the foul lines of our own choices. That is why, if we wish to be truly happy and fulfilled, we must do all we can to make the right choices. We must want the right things.

We must also want the things we can have.

Of course, this does not mean we should never try to reach beyond what we are or the things we have today. It does not mean that we should not challenge ourselves, strive to excel, become better people, and live richer, fuller lives. What it does mean is that we must always be careful only to reach for the things that matter, that we must work to focus our lives on the things that not only count but that make a difference when we do attain them. These are most often the simple things in life. And it is astonishing how readily attainable they are. Jesus Himself gave us the formula: "But seek ye first the kingdom of God, and his righteousness; and all these things shall be added unto you" (Matthew 6:33).

What do you want? What will make you happy? A million dollars? Popularity? To be accepted by the "right people"? To distinguish yourself in academia? Can you have those things? I don't know. I don't know if you will make a million dollars, attain the popularity, acceptance, and all the "right" friends, or reach the academic heights of which you dream. But I know some things you can have without a doubt. Here's one: "Blessed are they which do hunger and thirst after righteousness: for they shall be filled" (Matthew 5:6). If you want a relationship with God, you can have it. If you want to walk with Him, you can. If you want the righteousness, peace, and joy found in the Holy Ghost, you can have them. You can go as high in God, as deep in God, as far with God as you want to go.

If you want the things of this world, you might attain them or you might not. But if you want the things of God, there is not a devil big enough, there's not a circumstance bad enough, there's not a problem tough enough to keep you from reaching them.

Psalm 37:4 is a discussion of this very issue: "Delight thyself

*T*rust in the LORD, and do good; so shalt thou dwell in the land, and verily thou shalt be fed.

Delight thyself also in the LORD; and he shall give thee the desires of thine heart.

Commit thy way unto the LORD; trust also in him; and he shall bring it to pass (Psalm 37:3-5).

also in the LORD; and he shall give thee the desires of thine heart." I have often heard this verse explained to mean that if we choose to do His will in our lives, then He will give us whatever we desire in our hearts. Once again, the philosophy is, "If I do my part, God will do His part." There are many problems with this interpretation besides the obvious cheapening of our love and devotion and turning God into nothing more than a great Santa Claus in the sky.

In living by this concept, we see our relationship with God as no more than action and reaction: put in the money, and out comes the cold drink. My service to Him becomes no more than the payment I have to make to get the things I want.

The biggest problem with this philosophy is that we know it isn't true. Life just doesn't work like that. We know that good things happen to bad people, and bad things happen to good people. There are many who delight in the Lord who have sickness, financial troubles, family problems; surely those things are not their hearts' desire.

What then, does this verse of Scripture mean? Look at it again. What if "delight thyself also in the LORD" doesn't mean just to dutifully do what God wants us to do so that we can get our reward as good boys and girls? What if it means to really enjoy walking with Him, to enjoy being in His presence not to get a reward, but just because we love Him, because it is our delight, and because it makes us happy?

Then the meaning is entirely different. The psalmist was saying that if our desire is Him, if He is what makes us happy, then He will guarantee that we will be happy, for we can have Him.

He will not guarantee us a million dollars, a life without pain and sorrow, acceptance by all the right people, or the thousand other things we decide are necessary for our happiness. But if what we want above all things is to know Him, to walk with Him, and to serve Him, He does promise us that that desire will be fulfilled.

This is the consolation Paul offered us when he wrote,

> *Who shall separate us from the love of Christ? shall tribulation, or distress, or persecution, or famine, or nakedness, or peril, or sword? As it is written, For thy sake we are killed all the day long; we are accounted as sheep for the slaughter. Nay, in all these things we are more than conquerors through him that loved us. For I am persuaded, that neither death, nor life, nor angels, nor principalities, nor powers, nor things present, nor things to come, nor height, nor depth, nor any other creature, shall be able to separate us from the love of God, which is in Christ Jesus our Lord* (Romans 8:35-39).

THE CONTEST

Leah's obsession led to a tragic contention between her and her sister that defined much of the remainder of their lives. It began almost immediately after that first awful morning when Jacob stormed from the tent to demand that Laban live up to their agreement and give him Rachel as his wife.

From the beginning, the conflict centered around their children. In that day, bearing children was the highest contribution a woman could make to her family. Consequently, her value as a person was unalterably connected to her having children. The contest for Jacob's love would take place on this battlefield.

Leah seemed to be the early winner. She bore Jacob a son right away, probably in the first year. Rachel did not. In fact, as Leah continued to bear children, it became evident that Rachel was barren. Rachel agonized over this, even though giving Jacob children did not seem to give Leah any advantage. Not even four sons enabled Leah to win her husband's love. In anguish, Rachel rather illogically went to Jacob and demanded that he give her children, too. It seems obvious that while she undoubtedly wanted children for all the usual reasons, she was also frustrated by her sister's fruitful womb. Jacob's reaction revealed the frustration he too was feeling: "Can I take the place of God, who has denied you children?" (Genesis 30:2, *NEB*).

Rachel's response to her circumstance was to escalate the tension; she gave her handmaiden to Jacob as his third wife. This makes sense only when we recognize that in a strange way, that long-ago culture credited Rachel with providing children to her husband by giving him the servant girl. In this light, Bilhah, Rachel's handmaiden, was more like a surrogate mother than a true wife for Jacob. Because of this, she would not occupy the same standing in the family as Leah and Rachel. Obviously, though, she would compete with both of them for Jacob's notice.

There is no question that by giving Bilhah to Jacob, Rachel was striving for an advantage over Leah. When Bilhah bore Jacob a son we read, "And Rachel said, With great wrestlings have I wrestled with my sister, and I have prevailed: and she called his name Naphtali" (Genesis 30:8).

Rachel's motive was not lost on Leah; she was threatened by Rachel's dramatic gambit. Bilhah was young, strong, perhaps beautiful, and worse, her children would enhance Rachel's standing with Jacob and the community. This would never do! So Leah retaliated with a desperate ploy of her own: she gave Jacob her handmaiden, too. This girl's name was Zilpah, and like Rachel's surrogate Bilhah, she would give Jacob two sons.

The giving of the two handmaidens to Jacob as wives, while dramatic, was not unusual. In fact, it was exactly what Sarah did when it seemed she could not bear Abraham a child. Her handmaiden, Hagar, bore Ishmael. There was tension between Sarah and Hagar, too, which ultimately led to Hagar and Ishmael being banished by Abraham.

Now there were four wives. Leah had three competitors for Jacob's time and attention. One of them Jacob loved with almost a fairy-tale love. The writer gave no real indication of Jacob's feelings for Bilhah and Zilpah. Probably his feelings for them were over-shadowed by his love for Rachel.

But there was only one of his wives of whom it was said, "Leah was hated."

BLESSED

And when the LORD saw that Leah was hated, he opened her womb: but Rachel was barren (Genesis 29:31).

CHAPTER 4

LOVE AND BLESSINGS

Leah was tragically cheated, and the consequences of it would last her entire lifetime. Her life story would be nothing but a study in frustration, she becoming only an object of our pity except for one astonishing fact: even though she suffered this terrible tragedy, the Lord loved Leah. This runs contrary to popular belief about the nature of God's love and its relationship to His blessings. We think that if God loves us His blessings will fill our life, and that means everything will always go well. The sorrow, disappointment, and pain with which others struggle will not touch us. If this is what we believe, how can we reconcile Leah's circumstances with the plain statement of the Lord's blessings on her life? How could Leah be in such a spiteful, interminable situation while the Lord was "blessing" her? Why would the Lord allow this to happen to someone whom He loved?

Please understand one thing: *we cannot gauge the love of God by the circumstances of our life.* God loves us on our worst day, just like He loves us on our best day. No matter how bad it gets, no matter how unfair life is, no matter how unjust our circumstances, no matter how much we have been cheated, one thing is certain: God's love is constant. God's love is unchanging. When things are good, He loves us. When things are bad, He loves us still.

God loved Leah and expressed His love, not by removing all the unfair circumstances from her life, but by blessing her in spite of them. The wonderful thing is, the Bible indicates that He seemed to love her more because of what she had gone through. The Scripture says that when He saw that she was hated, the Lord loved her and the Lord blessed her.

Paul also struggled with the seeming contradiction of this aspect of God's love. He knew himself to be a chosen vessel; his life was blessed in a magnificent way. At the same time, though, he was stricken with a serious health problem that threatened his ministry. Paul called it his "thorn in the flesh." Many scholars believe it was a disease of the eyes that affected Paul's sight, which is why many of his letters were dictated. Maybe this also explains why in one of those letters, or epistles, in which Paul did write a small passage with his own hand, he called attention to the hand-writing, saying he was writing with "large letters," giving the impression, at least to many, that he could not see to write normally. Whatever the problem was, he asked God to heal it.

And God said no.

Paul asked again, and God said no again.

The third time Paul prayed for healing, God answered him with an explanation of His refusal to heal: "My strength," He said, "is made perfect in weakness" (II Corinthians 12:9).

God was telling Paul that our weaknesses, our pain, our problems are not meant to destroy us. Instead, they are opportunities God uses to weave His strength into the fabric of our lives. Just as the glue that holds a broken cup together is stronger than the cup itself, the strength of God in the weakest parts of our lives is by far the strongest part of us, stronger than our greatest strength.

Paul and Leah were not alone in their struggle with God's penchant for blessing in one area of our lives while leaving untouched the pain in another. The psalmist shared his confusion brought about by his observations of the world around him:

But as for me, my feet were almost gone; my steps had well nigh slipped. For I was envious at the foolish, when I saw the prosperity of the wicked. . . . Verily I have cleansed my heart in vain, and washed my hands in innocency (Psalm 73:2-3, 13).

The writer saw great injustice in life. The wicked prospered while the righteous suffered. When he considered his own choice to please God and to endeavor to do right, he felt that surely he had wasted his time cleansing his heart and washing his hands. It just seemed to reap no benefit. What good did it do to choose right over wrong if that choice caused life to get worse instead of better? As he strove to serve God, this question loomed ever larger in his thoughts, until it was "too painful" for him (Psalm 73:16). He testified that the injustice he saw everywhere brought such turmoil to his soul that he had almost given up: "But as for me, my feet were almost gone; my steps had well nigh slipped" (Psalm 73:2).

But visiting the sanctuary of God, and sitting in God's presence, enabled him to look beyond the injustice all around him and to see past his disappointment and pain to realize that fair and unfair cannot be calculated until the whole story is known. Only when we see all the way down the road to the end can we know the true result of any condition or circumstance. When the psalmist saw the end of the unrighteous who prospered in spite of their evil, he understood the true nature of blessing and cursing:

Then understood I their end. Surely thou didst set them in slippery places: thou castedst them down into destruction. How are they brought into desolation, as in a moment! they are utterly consumed with terrors. . . . For, lo, they that are far from thee shall perish. . . . But it is good for me to draw near to God (Psalm 73:17-19, 27, 28).

BLESSED REGARDLESS

Sometimes what happens to us is the result of our own actions. Bad choices, wrong decisions, and careless attitudes all take their toll and exact from us their own price for our mistakes. Although not a popular philosophy in our day, an era in which victimhood has been elevated to unprecedented heights, we have no one to blame for this suffering but ourselves. God doesn't bring these results on us; we bring them on ourselves. The antidote is discipline, maturity, counsel, and wisdom. Our lives are made better by making better choices.

However, sometimes what happens to us is not the result of any choices we made or actions we took. Sometimes we not only don't get what we deserve; we get what we don't deserve. The great frustration is that we cannot often change those circumstances. Since nothing we did caused them, nothing we do can change them.

Of course, I do not mean to minimize the power of prayer and faith. God does sometimes intervene, reverse circumstances, and give us what we call a miracle. He heals, delivers, and restores, and

So went Satan forth from the presence of the Lord, and smote Job with sore boils from the sole of his foot unto his crown. And he took him a potsherd to scrape himself withal; and he sat down among the ashes. Then said his wife unto him, Dost thou still retain thine integrity? curse God, and die. But he said unto her, Thou speakest as one of the foolish women speaketh. What? shall we receive good at the hand of God, and shall we not receive evil? In all this did not Job sin with his lips (Job 2:7-10).

because He does, we approach life not with dread but with hope. We know that all things are possible with God. But we also know that sometimes He does not choose to change things. This is what troubled the psalmist, this is what troubled Paul, and it troubles us, too.

In these times we find ourselves being tested. How will we allow these injustices to affect us? What will we do when we've been cheated? Will we grow bitter, angry, and resentful that things are not different? Or will we, like Job, trust God in spite of circumstance? Can we believe that God loves us and is blessing us, even though not everything in our lives is the way we would wish it to be?

What do we do when things are really going bad? What is the antidote for our frustration when we are having a really bad day, when everything seems to be working against us? One important and effective action is to follow the steps of the writer of Psalm 73: go to the house of God. Don't sit at home feeling sorry for yourself. Don't even languish in the last pew; go on up to the front. Join in the worship and praise, tap into the joy of those around you, open your heart to the preached Word. There you, like the psalmist, will be able to see beyond the dreary present. With hope rekindled, you will find courage to face the day. When things are wrong, you can be certain that God is going to find a way to bless you, even in the middle of your struggle. Life is unfair, but God loves you. Life is unjust, but God will bless you.

God blessed Leah. Although He did not remove the unfairness from her life, He blessed her nevertheless. And He blessed her in the most significant way possible: He opened her womb and gave her children.

It is hard for us today to comprehend the full significance of Leah's blessing. Hers was a different time. Life was harsh. Survival required hard work and lots of hands to share it. It was important to have as many children as possible to work the fields and tend the flocks. Also, life was uncertain and family was the only source of security as old age approached. The only hope most people had was that their children would care for them when they could no longer support themselves.

The result of these hard facts was a society where women had one purpose in life above all others: to give birth. It was in bringing children into the world that women found meaning and purpose. Because male children were stronger and could provide better security for their parents' old age, it was even more important that wives produce male children. The culture awarded and encouraged this in a simple way: a woman who bore children, particularly male children, was honored. In fact, it was the highest honor.

Rachel basked in her husband's love. Jacob choked up when she walked into a room. He spoke words to her that he could never bring himself to speak to Leah. He looked at her in a way that he would never look at Leah. But Rachel was barren.

The Lord saw Leah, who was the victim of a great injustice and who, through no fault of her own, was condemned to a life of rejection and strife. She had done nothing to deserve her husband's cold disdain. Hated by her husband, resented by her sister, used as a pawn in her father's selfish schemes, she had been condemned to an unvalued, purposeless life. Then God blessed her, and she bore Jacob his first son. He continued to bless her until, eventually, Leah gave Jacob six of his twelve sons. His other three wives gave him only two each. Leah was the most fruitful wife, the greatest blessing to the family. Again and again, God showed His love and His blessing toward Leah in the most significant way that He could. He gave her sons.

MISUSED BLESSINGS

And Leah conceived, and bare a son, and she called his name Reuben: for she said, Surely the LORD hath looked upon my affliction; now therefore my husband will love me. And she conceived again, and bare a son; and said, Because the LORD hath heard that I was hated, he hath therefore given me this son also: and she called his name Simeon. And she conceived again, and bare a son; and said, Now this time will my husband be joined unto me, because I have born him three sons: therefore was his name called Levi (Genesis 29:32-34).

CHAPTER 5

FORCING LIFE TO BE FAIR

God showed His love for Leah by opening her womb and giving her children. Unfortunately, Leah had become obsessed with one thing in life. She was so driven to win the love of her husband that she misread, misinterpreted, and even misused the blessings of God. Instead of recognizing them as a sign of His love, given in spite of the circumstances of her life, Leah saw her blessings as tools to use. Instead of proof of God's unchanging love, she saw only what she thought was a way to make life fair.

I believe we can understand and sympathize. When they laid her first-born son in her arms, she counted his fingers and toes and marveled at how perfect he was. Beyond that, she saw only one thing. "Now," she said, "my husband will love me." Leah thought, *Now I will get what I deserve. Now life will be fair.*

She named the baby *Reuben*, which means "see me."

We can have no doubt about the message she was sending Jacob by naming his son that. The agony she felt every time she saw Jacob and Rachel together and how he looked at Rachel was raw and real. Now, she was convinced that this baby would change all that. She thought, *He won't ignore me now that I have given him his first son.*

Now he will look at me the way he looks at her. When I walk into the room, his eyes will follow me, as they once followed her. Now, this time . . . my husband will love me.

But even though she gave him his first child, Jacob did not fall in love with her. He exulted in his new son but continued to ignore the baby's mother. His eyes still lit up when Rachel entered the room and darkened when Leah came near.

Unfortunately, Leah's efforts did not work for her, and such attempts will not work for us. We can try to put the blessings of God on display to show everyone how much God loves us; we can use them in an attempt to force others to recognize our worth, but in the end it will be for naught. We cannot force someone to love us; we cannot make life fair in all situations. Some problems, I am sorry to say, we just cannot fix.

Leah's need to win Jacob's love was so insistent and her obsession so powerful that she could not bring herself to give up. When her second child was born, another boy, she named him *Simeon*, which means "hear me." She still did not change Jacob's feelings for her. When her third son was born, she named him *Levi*, which means "join me." She said, "Now my husband is going to join me because I have given him three boys and Rachel has given him none." But still nothing changed.

She tried again and again. Son after son. I don't know how long

We cannot change people. Any attempts to control them are a delusion as well as an illusion. People will either resist our efforts or redouble their efforts to prove we can't control them. They may temporarily adapt to our demands, but the moment we turn our backs they will return to their natural state. Furthermore, people will punish us for making them do something they don't want to do, or be something they don't want to be. No amount of control will effect a permanent or desirable change in another person. We can sometimes do things that increase the probability that people will want to change, but we can't even guarantee or control that.

And that's the truth. It's too bad. It's sometimes hard to accept, especially if someone you love is hurting him or herself and you. But that's the way it is. The only person you can now or ever change is yourself. The only person that it is your business to control is yourself.

—Melody Beattie

Codependent No More: How to Stop Controlling Others and Start Caring for Yourself she continued to hope. How long did she compete with Rachel? How long was everything about trying to gain Jacob's love? How long did she live every aspect of her life, including the bringing of children into the world, in a way designed only to make life fair and thereby to finally end her suffering? How long? Five years? Ten years? I don't know how long, but I know this: Leah finally came to the crossroads of her life.

Sooner or later we all arrive at the place where we must make a momentous decision: whether our life is going to be one long struggle against the injustice and unfairness of our circumstances; whether we are going to let those times when we are cheated make us bitter, angry, and full of resentment because we didn't get what we deserved. We must decide whether we are going to allow life to defeat us, destroy us, and condemn us to end our days embittered by our painful experiences, or whether we are going to take a higher path, walk a higher road, and focus our lives away from what we didn't get, what we don't have, and what didn't happen and toward the many wonderful things God has done for us.

I am not talking about a resigned, doormat attitude about the obstacles that lay astride our path. It is right to strive to overcome injustice and to resist its evil presence in our lives, but we must not allow that struggle to cause us to miss the joy of life, the peace of recognizing the constant love of God, and the thankfulness we should feel for the many good things He showers on us each day. Leah was so focused on winning the battle for her husband's love that she missed seeing the love of God expressed all around her. Her children's very names—"See me!" "Hear me!" "Join me!"— were a constant reminder of her emptiness and the futility of her struggle to be loved and accepted. The great tragedy of her story is that these children whose names defined Leah's self-absorption were, all the while, the living proof that she was already loved and already accepted. Her obsession blinded her.

I remember once meeting a couple who were very active and very much engaged with their church. They had been extremely blessed in business but now were retired and wished to spend their remaining days serving the kingdom in any way they could. They *had* blessed the kingdom in so many ways. I both admired them and felt sorry for them. I admired their dedication and generous spirit. But I was saddened by their need, so easy to see after only a few minutes of conversation, to use their wealth (God's blessings) as proof of their personal value and their Christianity. "See," they seemed to be saying, "notice all these things we have done. Don't they prove we are good people? Don't they show we are worthy of love?" It was painfully obvious that they did not act out of a genuine concern for others' need of help and need of God but performed their deeds out of their own need to be loved and accepted. They were misusing God's blessings.

We all act out of self-interest occasionally; it is a human trait that the Bible recognized: "For all seek their own, not the things which are Jesus Christ's" (Philippians 2:21).

It is certainly true that much good is done by people who do those good things only to be appreciated or applauded, and good is often accomplished by those who act out of even more selfish agendas. The apostle Paul recognized this fact.

> *Some indeed preach Christ even of envy and strife; and some also of good will: the one preach Christ of contention, not sincerely, supposing to add affliction to my bonds: but the other of love, knowing that I am set for the defence of the gospel. What then? notwithstanding, every way, whether in pretence, or in truth, Christ is preached; and I therein do rejoice, yea, and will rejoice* (Philippians 1:15-18).

However, because good is sometimes done in spite of selfish motives, we should never be satisfied to be moved by these baser needs and impulses; our motives should be higher, purer. Jesus was asked about the motive behind His earthly ministry. His answer is well worth our study: "Even as the Son of man came not to be ministered unto, but to minister, and to give his life a ransom for many" (Matthew 20:28).

Why do our motives matter so much, especially if our actions result in good being accomplished? When we give to get or do good in order to be applauded, we not only rob ourselves of the real joy that comes from loftier motives, but we also reveal an inner emptiness, a hunger at the center of our heart. We admit, in our actions, an over-whelming desire to be loved and admired. The tragedy is that this emptiness, this desire, can never be filled no matter how much admiration we attract or applause we gain. Even if our cries of "see me! hear me! join me!" gain Jacob's glance, the thrill will not last, nor will it, in the end, satisfy.

This is why our service must be based on genuine love for our Master and His cause and for our fellowman. This is the only way to find true fulfillment, to fill the emptiness of our hearts.

With each passing day, Leah grew more frustrated and unhappy. Obviously, her efforts to gain Jacob's love had failed. He loved their children, but his feelings for her had not changed. Rachel could still stop him in his tracks by just walking into the room, but he didn't seem to realize Leah existed.

Then, when the birth of Levi ("Join me!") seemed to make

no difference in Leah's relationship with Jacob, something else began to change. This change was not in her circumstances or in Jacob or in Rachel; her world did not change. Instead, change came to Leah herself.

THIS TIME, PRAISE

And she conceived again, and bare a son: and she said, Now will I praise the LORD: therefore she called his name Judah; and left bearing (Genesis 29:35).

CHAPTER 6

JUDAH

Leah was expecting her fourth child. This time, as the babe grew in her womb, a new attitude grew in her heart. Perhaps Leah had come to recognize the futility of her long struggle to gain Jacob's love. Maybe the grace of God's love, blessing her even when she had failed to appreciate the true meaning of His blessings, finally broke through the walls of her obsession. Or maybe Leah finally tired of the never-successful effort and decided it was time to move on. Whatever her motive, the Bible teaches that when this little boy came along, something happened within Leah that changed everything.

When they laid the baby in her arms, she counted his fingers and toes and looked long into his face. Then with an air of decision she spoke to those around her. "This time I don't care whether Jacob ever loves me or not. I am going to quit living my life trying to force everything to be fair. From today onward I'm refusing to be dominated by what's wrong in my life. This time I am going to get it right. This time I am going to lift my eyes." And she called his name *Judah*, which means "praise."

"This time," she said, "I am going to praise God."

To praise means to express approval or admiration, to offer grateful homage.

Praise to God is lifting up and glorifying the Lord. It is centering our attention upon Him with heartfelt expressions of love, adoration, and thanksgiving. Praise connects us to the supernatural and invokes the power of God. Miracles happen when we praise.

We praise God in many ways: with our voices in words and singing, with our skill in playing musical instruments; we also praise Him in shouting, dancing, lifting or clapping our hands. True praise is a joining of the human heart and the Spirit of God. "God is a Spirit: and they that worship him must worship him in spirit and in truth" (John 4:24).

Praise is more than what happens at church, however. Praise should be a part of our lifestyle. Everywhere we go—home, work, at the mall, at school—a heart filled with praise brings joy and victory to us. His power and anointing accompany even silent praise when offered from a sincere, focused heart. "I will bless the LORD at all times: his praise shall continually be in my mouth" (Psalm 34:1).

Praise is a declaration of our faith and trust. It expresses our belief that God is with us, and regardless of the circumstances in which we find ourselves, He will see us through. "By him therefore let us offer the sacrifice of praise to God continually, that is, the fruit of our lips giving thanks to his name" (Hebrews 13:15).

This change of focus, away from herself and her problems and onto a gracious God who loved her and accepted her, changed everything. Jacob came in, walked to the bed, and gently picked up his newborn son. "What's his name?" he asked. She looked up from the bed, and their eyes locked. She said, "His name is Praise."

Leah's declaration of freedom could not have been lost on Jacob. It was surely obvious that something had fundamentally changed. The unspoken words were clear, telegraphed between them by the pronouncement of the baby's name. He must have understood: "It is not about me this time, Jacob, and it's surely not about you. This time it is about Him. I finally woke up and realized where my blessings have come from. I know now where the love that I need in my life is to be found, I know where my worth is, where my value as a human being rests. I finally realize what life is all about. God loves me. He cares about me. As for you, Jacob, keep looking at Rachel with that look you reserve only for her. Speak to her with those words you save only for her. I accept that I will never see that look or hear those words, but that fact will no longer control me. From here on, I am going to praise the Lord."

I have a simple message for you. When life cheats you, there is an antidote. It seems too simple to be effective, but it has the power to change everything. When life is unfair, when you've been cheated, turn from your pain and disappointment and turn toward God with a heart of praise. When everything is against you, change your focus. When nothing is going right, lift your eyes a little higher. This time see life in a whole new way.

"This time I will praise the Lord. This time I will get it right."

ACCEPTED IN THE BELOVED

In Paul's majestic *berakah* (blessing) of Ephesians 1, he used a phrase that arrests one's attention: "To the praise of the glory of his grace, wherein he hath made us accepted in the beloved" (Ephesians 1:6). Accepted in the beloved!

Our value as a human being is not based on what others may think of us or whether we are accepted into one group or another. Our worth is not based on standards of accomplishment or in secular definitions of success. Our value as a person is based on our relationship with Jesus Christ. This is the one standard that is unaffected by circumstances; no matter how life has treated us, whether good or bad, fair or unfair, we are accepted in Him.

This acceptance is based on our praise for Him. This is why He saved us through the power of the new birth, that we might praise Him.

But ye are a chosen generation, a royal priesthood, an holy nation, a peculiar people; that ye should shew forth the praises of him who hath called you out of darkness into his marvellous light (I Peter 2:9).

By fulfilling this purpose, we find purpose and meaning in our lives. Free of the frustration of always reaching and never grasping, we find the peace that surpasses circumstances, transcends our troubles, and brings a quiet confidence in the face of life's worst storms.

Praise means celebrating God. Undoubtedly you have seen, and probably participated in, celebrations like Fourth of July fireworks displays and Memorial Day parades. The purpose of such festivities is not simply to set off firecrackers and Roman candles or to watch graying veterans march down city streets. The events are held to remember and honor the sacrifices of men and women who went before and paid the price for freedom. As Christians, our lives are living tributes to God's grace. God selected us as believers so that we might praise Him. When others look at our lives, what kinds of "tributes" do they see? Liberated, engaging individuals, full of gratitude for all He has done for us? Or shriveled, sullen, embittered shells that feel as though we've been cheated out of life's good things? Let your prayer life and worship express your gratitude to God.[2]

THIS TIME, PRAISE

In discovering this truth about praise, Leah unlocked something within herself that swelled in praise toward God, and in that praise she found liberty.

Praise is the doorway to a new life. Crossing the threshold of praise is the first step to a new attitude, a new outlook, and a new purpose. In praise our eyes are lifted to new vistas in every direction, stretching to the horizon as far as we can see. We cannot dwell on the negatives in our lives when our eyes are lifted in praise. "I will lift up mine eyes unto the hills," the psalmist sang, "from whence cometh my help" (Psalm 121:1).

We have all looked toward distant horizons to relieve the stress of our day. I remember driving through the Ozarks on a particularly trying day during an extremely difficult time. Even though it was a beautiful fall afternoon, I was so wrapped in gloom that I hardly saw anything around me. Then, rounding a curve, I saw a majestic view of a steep hillside covered by trees displaying leaves with the most beautiful reds, yellows, and golds I had ever seen. The scene was breathtaking. Suddenly, tears filled my eyes and gratitude swelled my heart, as I could not escape the feeling—silly, I know—that God had dressed that hillside in such beautiful garments just for me, to lift my spirits and assure me of His understanding and love. The fervent praise for Him and thankfulness for His love lifted my spirits.

Maybe this was what Leah felt when she took her fourth son in her arms. Maybe her heart swelled for the first time with an overwhelming sense of thankfulness. For the first time, she was thankful not that she had another weapon in her fight to force life to be fair, but for her baby, a love-gift from God, an expression of His acceptance of her, regardless of her circumstances.

Just as pausing to take in a beautiful view lifts our spirits and gives us a new perspective, so does taking our eyes from our struggles and looking to our blessings give us new understanding of the inexpressible beauty of His unfailing love.

Some would say that living a life of peace and joy is to surrender to circumstance. They believe that we must constantly battle life, refusing to relax, ever. Did Leah, then, really just give up, surrender to her circumstances, and live in denial by losing herself in praise? Not at all. Leah finally recognized that she could never end her pain through her by now years-long struggle to change the people in her life. All that struggle had accomplished was to allow those other people to control her by their refusal to change. Far from giving up, she had found the path to ultimate victory.

The kind of praise that changes lives goes far beyond what we do or say in church. While, of course, our public, verbal worship and praise are an integral part of the process and should never be neglected, the true power of praise is brought to bear by the praise that is embedded in the heart. It goes beyond the action of the moment and becomes a lifestyle. When praise lifts the eyes not just for the moment but for a lifetime, circumstances no longer dictate our responses. We stop being a victim once and for all.

How does such a complete change occur? It begins with the change that is so fundamental that Jesus called it being "born again." A Jewish rabbi named Nicodemus approached Jesus one night with an implied question about the purpose of Jesus' ministry. "Rabbi," he began, "we know you are a man come from God, because no one could do the miracles you do if that weren't true." Jesus went immediately to the heart of His purpose: "Except a man be born again, he cannot see the kingdom of God." When Nicodemus did not understand and asked how a man could be born a second time, Jesus made it clearer: "Except a man be born of water and of the

Spirit, he cannot enter into the kingdom of God" (John 3:5).

The new-birth message was made clearest when Peter answered the people who, when they were touched by his declaration that Jesus Christ was Lord, asked, "What must we do?"

Then Peter said unto them, Repent, and be baptized every one of you in the name of Jesus Christ for the remission of sins, and ye shall receive the gift of the Holy Ghost (Acts 2:38).

Through the baptism of the Holy Spirit and baptism in water in the name of Jesus, a new life begins. This new life is created by a whole new relationship with Christ: "For as many of you as have been baptized into Christ have put on Christ" (Galatians 3:27). Paul described it to the Corinthians: "Therefore if any man be in Christ, he is a new creature: old things are passed away; behold, all things are become new" (II Corinthians 5:17). This change, though it begins with definite experiences and is apparent immediately, is the work not just of a moment but of a lifetime.

Life began for Leah when she began to praise the Lord.

HAPPY EVER AFTER

And he charged them, and said unto them, I am to be gathered unto my people: bury me with my fathers in the cave that is in the field of Ephron the Hittite, in the cave that is in the field of Machpelah, which is before Mamre, in the land of Canaan, which Abraham bought with the field of Ephron the Hittite for a possession of a buryingplace. There they buried Abraham and Sarah his wife; there they buried Isaac and Rebekah his wife; and there I buried Leah (Genesis 49:29-31).

CHAPTER 7

LIFETIME OF CHANGE

So what happened when Leah discovered the power of praise? Like most real-life stories, there is no simple ending, no "happily ever after." Leah was changed, no doubt about that. Her commitment to reclaiming her sense of self-worth by focusing on God slowly transformed her. That doesn't mean there were no problems and struggles. Life did not suddenly become "fair" when she started worshiping God. As far as the record is concerned, Jacob never looked at her in the same way he looked at Rachel. He never said the things to Leah that he said to Rachel. None of that changed.

There were still problems between Leah and Rachel. For a long time, things were no easier. The change that came to Leah when she lifted her eyes toward God was not immediately reflected in the circumstances of her outward life. At least in the beginning, the change was only on the inside of her spirit and soul.

The struggle with Rachel not only continued but for a time grew worse. The handmaidens were given to Jacob even after the birth of Judah. The incident that found Leah trading Reuben's mandrakes for a night with her husband happened even later. But there were subtle changes in Leah from the time of Judah's birth. It is true that when Zebulun, her sixth and last son was born, she said, "Now will my husband live with me," but even that showed a shift in attitude, as if Leah had begun to recognize and accept her place in Jacob's household.

Eventually, her change of heart began to produce a change in demeanor. And as Leah changed, a slow change came to Jacob and Leah's relationship. Maybe not love, but respect began to grow in Jacob's heart.

After thirteen years of living in Laban's shadow, Jacob determined to leave. When God spoke to him, Jacob knew the time had come. He was in the field with his sheep when he made up his mind. He wanted advice and the assurance that his family was supportive of his decision, so he asked Rachel and Leah to meet him in order to discuss leaving their home and father. It is significant that he called for both Rachel and Leah, not just Rachel. Leah had won a place in her husband's eyes that she had not had before she began to praise the Lord, the place that she had not had when she was trying desperately to win his love. As the years passed, quietness came over Leah. As the peace of God formed in her heart, she made peace with both her place and with the people in her family.

In all, Leah bore Jacob six sons, Reuben, Simeon, Levi,

Judah, Issachar, and Zebulun, and at least one daughter, Dinah. Eventually Rachel's prayers were answered; her womb was opened, and she bore two sons, Joseph and Benjamin. Each of the handmaidens also gave Jacob two sons. It is interesting that God's blessings on Leah were made obvious in that she gave Jacob half of his twelve sons.

The escape from Padan-aram was traumatic as Laban pursued Jacob and his family. It could have ended in conflict and even bloodshed had Laban not been warned in a dream to treat his son-in-law with respect. In the end, Laban pronounced a wary blessing on Jacob's return to Canaan.

The harrowing reunion with Esau must have been a terrifying ordeal, but in the middle of it, Jacob had his own encounter with God and more than his name was changed.

No tragedy of his life marked Jacob more than when Benjamin was born in a small shepherd's village called Bethlehem, because, in giving birth to Benjamin, Rachel died. Jacob buried his beloved wife in a beautiful sepulcher he built for her there.

The Bible does not tell us how long Leah survived Rachel. It was very probably many years. Finally, most likely as an elderly grandmother, Leah died. There is no record of Jacob's immediate reaction to her death. We do know there was no special sarcophagus built for Leah, no beautiful monument to commemorate her life. Instead, Jacob took her body to the cave at Machpelah, the burial place of his grandfather, grandmother, father, and mother, and buried her there.

More eventful years passed. Joseph was sold into slavery by his brothers, who deceived Jacob into believing that Joseph had been killed by a wild animal. He carried this grief for years until famine forced his sons to approach the regent of Egypt for corn only to discover that the regent was Joseph. Jacob and his entire household moved to Egypt to be under Joseph's protection during the hard times. There, in Egypt, death came for Jacob.

BURY ME

As his death neared, the old patriarch summoned his sons, along with two of his grandsons, to his deathbed. When they had gathered, he began to speak his final words. First, he prophesied over his sons, predicting their futures and describing their roles and those of their descendants in God's plan for the nation He would build. One by one, sometimes bluntly, sometimes tenderly, he described their strengths and weakness and how those traits would determine each of their destinies.

Finally, Jacob's strength waned and his voice failed. His breathing grew shallow and slow, the death rattle already in his throat. His last words were raspy and barely audible. All fourteen men wept as they leaned near, listening, straining to hear every word. He whispered, "I am about to be gathered to my people. Bury me . . ." I have no doubt that they thought they knew what he was going to say. They were already planning the long trip back to the shepherd's village, Bethlehem, to that beautiful mausoleum that Jacob had built in memory of his lovely and deeply loved Rachel. They thought he would want to be with her, and they were already thinking of the logistics of getting his body there. But his words put an abrupt end to their silent planning. They were shocked when he said, "Bury me with my fathers in the cave." Maybe Jacob sensed their surprise and confusion, so to make sure that they understood, he summoned his last reserve of strength and spoke his final words: "Because there I buried Leah."

How could it be that the last word that slipped from Jacob's lips was the name of a woman he did not love? Could it be that when Jacob thought about life, he thought about Rachel, but when he thought of eternity, he thought of the light in those weak eyes of Leah, the light that came the day little Judah was born? When he thought about forever, he thought about Leah.

In the end, after all the struggle and pain, Leah's dream came true: her husband finally joined her. For thousands of years to come, Rachel would lie alone in her beautiful tomb at Bethlehem, but in the cave at Machpelah would be Abraham and Sarah, Isaac and Rebekah, and with them Jacob . . . and Leah.

EPILOGUE

SAVING A NATION

The effects of Leah's choice to focus on God instead of her circumstances did not end with her death. The twelve sons of Jacob became the fathers of the twelve tribes of Israel. (Joseph was represented by his sons, Manasseh and Ephraim.) These twelve tribes played an important role in God's relationship with His chosen people. They will always represent the special bond between the Lord and His children; their names will appear in the twelve gates of the New Jerusalem.

Once the Egyptian slavery ended, the twelve tribes became one nation. After the reigns of David and Solomon, the nation split in two, with the ten northern tribes taking the name of their ancestor, Jacob. The coalition was called Israel, the name God gave Jacob after he, like Leah, lifted his eyes from his struggle and saw God face-to-face. The two remaining tribes—one a son of Rachel: Benjamin, the other the son of Leah: Judah—united to form the southern nation that was called Judah. In 722 BC, Assyria destroyed Israel, and it disappeared from history. Eventually, Benjamin was absorbed into Judah and lost its separate identity. Thus, over the years, all the tribes but one disappeared. That tribe alone survived the ages. It was Judah, and Judah still exists to this day. We see this reflected in the fact that we still call the Hebrew people "Jews."

Leah's life did not make much difference when her focus was "see me," "hear me," or "join me." But when she changed her perspective and learned to live a life of praise, she helped to save a nation. That little boy, Judah, became the vehicle through which all of Jacob's descendants would endure for all time.

SAVING A WORLD

Even more significant, when God Himself became flesh and came into our world, He did not come through "see me," "hear me," or "join me," but He came as the Lion of the tribe of Judah. Jesus was not a descendant of the beautiful Rachel, as loved as she was, neither was He a descendant from either of the handmaids; He was a descendant of Leah.

By lifting her eyes from the unfairness of her circumstances, Leah not only changed her life, her marriage, and her family; she helped change the world.

It is a lesson well worth the learning that the more our lives focus on ourselves, the more our prayers are cries of "see me!" "hear me!" or "join me!" the less God can bless us and use us to bless others. It is only when we refocus our attention away from our circumstances and toward Him, it is only when we commit to making our lives a source of praise for Him that we open the unlimited possibilities He has in mind for each us.

Begin today, even in the midst of being cheated; join Leah in saying, "This time, I will praise the Lord."

ENDNOTES

[1]Richard Foster, *Freedom of Simplicity* (San Francisco: HarperSanFrancisco, 2005).

[2]*The Life Application Commentary Series* (Livingstone Corporation, with permission of Tyndale House Publishers, 1997, 1998, 1999, 2000).